'Any young person (who is or thinks they are PDA) reading it will learn so much about PDA, about themselves and about life. It's informative, supportive, practical and encouraging – but it's also fun too and it doesn't make any demands of its reader either. I absolutely adore this book!' – **Viv Dawes, autistic advocate and author of *Understanding Autistic Burnout***

'This guide has truly been a guiding light, providing invaluable support in my role as an emotional mentor. Navigating the intricate world of Pathological Demand Avoidance is no easy task, but this guide offers practical insights and strategies that make a world of difference. From deciphering triggers to fostering effective communication, this is a must-have for anyone seeking to better understand and empower teenagers with PDA.'
– Reece Archibald, mentor at MindJam

'How fantastic to have a neurodiversity-affirming resource to send PDAer teens to! Written in a voice which very obviously understands PDA and treads that difficult line of being accessible and teen-friendly without being patronising or unintentionally demanding – the best of both worlds.' – **Cathy Wassell, CEO Autistic Girls Network charity and author of *Nurturing Your Autistic Young Person***

'This book creates opportunities for young people to learn more about themselves and feel like they are not alone in how they think.'
– Chloe, social media influencer @Chloemejustme

'From the first moment I picked up this book, I couldn't put it down! I am 16 years old, and autistic (with a need for autonomy and self-directed learning), and everything in this book made so much sense. The book is written in a very friendly and conversational way, which demonstrates how great an understanding they have of autistic children (especially with PDA) and our needs.'
– Sam, producer and musician at Avid Beat

T0203345

By the same authors

The Educator's Experience of Pathological Demand Avoidance
An Illustrated Guide to Pathological
Demand Avoidance and Learning
Laura Kerbey
Illustrated by Eliza Fricker
ISBN 978 1 83997 696 4
eISBN 978 1 83997 698 8

The Family Experience of PDA
An Illustrated Guide to Pathological Demand Avoidance
Eliza Fricker
ISBN 978 1 78775 677 9
eISBN 978 1 78775 678 6

Can't Not Won't
A Story About a Child Who Couldn't Go to School
Eliza Fricker
ISBN 978 1 83997 520 2
eISBN 978 1 83997 521 9

Thumbsucker
An Illustrated Journey Through an
Undiagnosed Autistic Childhood
Eliza Fricker
ISBN 978 1 83997 854 8
eISBN 978 1 83997 855 5

The Teen's Guide to

Laura Kerbey

ILLUSTRATED BY ELIZA FRICKER

Foreword by Dr Julia Woollatt

Jessica Kingsley Publishers
London and Philadelphia

First published in Great Britain in 2024 by Jessica Kingsley Publishers
An imprint of John Murray Press

1

Copyright © Laura Kerbey 2024

Illustration copyright © Eliza Fricker 2024
Foreword copyright © Julia Woollatt 2024

A CIP catalogue record for this title is available from the British Library
and the Library of Congress

ISBN 978 1 80501 183 5
eISBN 978 1 80501 184 2

Printed and bound in Great Britain by TJ Books Ltd

Jessica Kingsley Publishers' policy is to use papers that are natural,
renewable and recyclable products and made from wood grown in
sustainable forests. The logging and manufacturing processes are expected
to conform to the environmental regulations of the country of origin.

Jessica Kingsley Publishers
Carmelite House
50 Victoria Embankment
London EC4Y 0DZ

www.jkp.com

John Murray Press
Part of Hodder & Stoughton Limited
An Hachette UK Company

This book is dedicated to all the amazing teenagers with PDA that I have had the pleasure of working with over the last 22 years. I truly believe that with the right support and understanding, you have the ability to make the world a better and more authentic place.

Particular thanks go to Alfie, Annie, Caitlin, Eliza, Micah, Rose and Sophie. I could not have written this book without your incredible insight and honesty.

CONTENTS

Foreword
Dr Julia Woollatt

I have worked with PDAers (autistic people with a profile of development and behaviour known as Pathological Demand Avoidance) and their families for many years as a clinical psychologist in community mental health teams, inpatient units, schools and private practice. During my time working with young people in the community, I met Laura and we worked with some of the same families and clients together. After I moved to private practice and was involved with the (now disbanded) PDA Development Group, my path crossed more frequently with Laura who, it became clearer to me, was (well, still is!) a driven neurodivergent woman with a passion for, and huge knowledge of, autism/PDA. I am now lucky enough to carry out assessments for autism and PDA with Laura for young people, as well as providing consultation and working on EOTAS/EOTIS (Education Other Than At/In School) packages. We continue to learn from each other and the incredible people we work with.

During my career, I have read numerous books and articles about PDA (increasing massively in number now, which is fantastic!), but one area that always seemed to be missed was teenage PDAers (who are a lot of the people I work with). This is the most amazing and inspiring group of young people, who often have so much to say and have a huge thirst for more knowledge about themselves/ others with a similar profile. Yet, despite this, there was nothing I felt I could recommend to support them with this, particularly that included the voices of young people themselves and was not too 'demanding'/theoretical/ boring (sorry to those who wrote those books!) or aimed at parents/carers, teachers or younger children. When Laura wrote, and Eliza illustrated, a brilliant book for teachers about PDA, I said to Laura that I just wished there was something like this for young people! And not much more than a year later, here I am being given the honour of writing the foreword for a book for young PDAers!

I'm going to be honest: teenagers and PDAers are probably some of the most challenging people to write a book for (come on, you know it's true – it's a tough crowd!) and yet Laura and Eliza have managed it. I'm not going to lie: it was hard, and I saw Laura experience 'writer's block' and avoid the demand of writing on many occasions, but together, they persevered. As a result, Laura and Eliza have written and illustrated an excellent book with honesty and humour, noting the challenges faced by, but also the strengths of, many of the young people we work with.

Laura and I are lucky enough to meet with many neurodivergent young people and their families, and we are constantly learning from them, which is why I am so pleased that their voices are so clearly heard in this book. Those who know Laura know she would never write this book without the voices of the people we work with being at the heart of it, but I am so proud (sorry for the praise, PDAers!) of the young people who contributed as they so articulately describe PDA, and I know this will be helpful to others. I know very well that not all PDAers will be able to read this book as, despite its brilliance, it may still be a demand, but for those who do, I think it will prove invaluable.

All that is left for me to say is that I hope you enjoy the book as much as I did (and I hope that it's not too much of a demand to read!). And if reading the whole book is too much of a demand – just skip the foreword and introduction like I normally do and head straight for the good stuff...or wait for the YouTube version!

I cannot wait to hear about how people find reading the book!

Julia

Acknowledgements

Thank you to my wonderful friend Eliza for her amazing illustrations. Once again, you have captured not just my words but the words and experiences of the teens who contributed to this book so simply yet so perfectly. I love the time we spend together writing, doodling, laughing, eating ice creams and dog spotting.

Thank you to my family, Steve, James and Fin, for putting up with me disappearing to write for hours on end and understanding my need to hyperfocus and be in my flow!

Thank you to the families of the teens who contributed to this book for helping us bring everything together.

Thank you to the team at JKP for your support and belief.

Introduction

During my career as an education and autism consultant, which has now spanned more than 20 years, I have had the pleasure of working with many children and young people with a PDA profile. As I confess in my first book, *The Educator's Experience of Pathological Demand Avoidance*, when you work in education, you are not meant to have favourites, but I do, and they almost all have PDA!

As part of my work, I offer consultations to parents of children with PDA, and also work with two multidisciplinary teams doing autism and PDA assessments. As part of this work, I am often asked for book recommendations, and although there are some brilliant books out there on PDA, there just didn't seem to be anything that I could recommend for teenagers who wanted to learn more about their PDA profile, or to parents or other professionals who worked with this cohort.

Although this book appeared to be much needed, it was not

easy to write! Understanding what I do about PDA, I had to find a way to carefully put my words, knowledge and advice down in a way that was honest, helpful and authentic, and not in any way patronizing or demanding to read.

The dreaded writer's block hit me on many occasions, but what helped me become unblocked was the amazing young people I interviewed who contributed to this book. They were simply brilliant, and I finished the writing process with an even greater understanding of the complexities of PDA thanks to them.

Now, if you are a parent of a teenager with a PDA profile, or a professional working with one, and you are reading this book, a word of cautionary advice: you will not be able to persuade your PDAer to read this book if they don't want to! Even just leaving it 'lying around' with the intention of it being picked up and read could be seen as a demand to read it. But I hope you find it a helpful insight into PDA and how you can support the young people in your care.

And if you are a PDAer reading this, then I know you are doing it because you want to and see the value in doing so, and I hope you too find it helpful as you navigate your teenage years and beyond.

Laura x

Welcome

Welcome to *The Teen's Guide to PDA*! This is your book, so you can read it in whatever way you want. It doesn't matter which order you read the chapters in, you can skip parts, come back to it, etc. You can write in it, scribble in it and doodle in it if you like too.

My name is Laura and I have worked with children and young people for more than 20 years. My friend Eliza is doing the illustrations for this book. She is a parent of a teenager with PDA. We have written other books together but realized that there was nothing out there for teenagers about PDA, so we decided to write this book for you.

Both Eliza and I are neurodivergent (I will explain what that means in Chapter 1 in case you don't know already).

The book has lots of quotes from other teenagers which help describe what it is like for them to live with PDA. You may relate to some of the comments but not all of them,

Welcome

and that is OK because every experience of PDA is different, and it doesn't mean their experiences are right and yours are wrong.

If you find it too demanding to read the whole book, you may find it helpful to just read the quotes and look at the illustrations rather than read the whole book.

Here is a little bit of information about the young people who have helped us with this book by contributing their experiences of PDA:

- Alfie is 15. He was diagnosed as autistic when he was 10 and then a year later with PDA. Alfie likes climbing, Dungeons and Dragons, blacksmithing, playing video games and the family dog. He dislikes large social gatherings, pompous idiots, yogurt and having PDA.

- Annie is 15 years old and was diagnosed with PDA when she was 11. Annie likes Sadie Sink, Taylor Swift, reading, horses and *The Office* (US version). She dislikes people who don't like Sadie Sink, the UK version of *The Office*, when a horse dies and when a record stops playing and you have to turn it over to continue playing.

- Caitlin is 17. She was diagnosed with PDA when she was 13. She is passionate about helping children and loves her dog Archie who is 2 (nearly 3). She loves DJing and has always loved music. She has always wanted to drive ever since she was young and always loved going on long car journeys. One of her main goals is to be a police officer.

- Eliza is now 18 and got a PDA diagnosis when she was 17. She likes music, clothes, creative things, reading, learning (but only on her own terms), octopuses, pirates, Alice in Wonderland and people and how they work. Eliza does not like boring things, living through boredom, being under-stimulated, struggling to find people like her, the colour yellow and doing anything she has even a tiny bit of apprehension or dislike for.

- Micah is 17 now and was diagnosed with autism when he was 11, and PDA shortly after. Micah loves cartoons and animation and the process of everything that goes into cartoons. He also loves music and music theory and analyzing what makes songs sound good. He also loves his boyfriend and clowns and dolls.

- Rose is 14 and was diagnosed with autism at 9 years old and PDA at 14. Rose likes cartoons, drawing, fashion and most insects, except crane flies (they freak her out!).

Being a teenager is a tricky time, anyway. Your body is changing and you have hormones raging around your body. People expect you to act like a grown-up at times, but then treat you like a kid, too! Adding PDA to the mix can make an already difficult time even harder! You may feel really misunderstood by others and may find it hard to understand yourself, too.

What we hope is that by reading this book you will have a better understanding of yourself, your amazing brain and why you are so good at some things but find other things tricky. We hope that it will help you to advocate for yourself better and explain to your family, friends and others what you need and don't need.

We hope you find this book helpful and can pick out the bits you need and are most relevant and beneficial to you. Most of all, we hope it doesn't feel too 'demandy' to read it!

Chapter 1

What Is PDA Anyway?

You might be reading this book because you have just been diagnosed with PDA, or Demand Avoidance, or perhaps you just want to know a little bit more about PDA.

One thing I am pretty sure of is that you are reading this because **you** want to know more about PDA, not because someone has told you to read it! If someone told you to read it, it would probably be in the bin or maybe the toilet!

PDA stands for Pathological Demand Avoidance. Some people prefer Pervasive or Persistent Drive for Autonomy, but we will come to that later in the book (if you like it and get that far!).

You may have also heard of PDA being used to describe 'Public Displays of Affection', but this is most definitely not a book about that! (Although I am sure those types of, ahem, books are available if you want to learn about that sort of thing as well.)

PDA is a profile of, or a type of, autism. The simplest way to describe PDA is that you have an anxiety-driven need to be in control and autonomous. Being autonomous means that you are self-driven and independent, and therefore you are in control. Having demands placed on you will feel very threatening and will make you feel anxious.

Demands can include:

- people telling you what to do
- people suggesting that you do things
- people expecting you to do things.

There are also self-imposed demands, so things that you yourself feel that you should or want to do.

> It is like a seesaw – you have the demand on one side and anxiety on the other. If your anxiety is really high [heavy], then the demand will be pushed up. If your anxiety is low [lighter], then the demand is easier. (Rose)

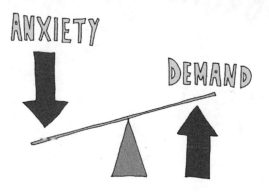

The more anxious you are, the harder demands will be to tolerate, and the less anxious you are, the easier demands will be.

If you have PDA or a PDA profile, then it means you are autistic. It also means that you are neurodivergent.

Being neurodivergent means that your brain works differently from a 'neurotypical' person's brain. Types of neurodiversity include:

DYSGRAPHIA

ADHD

DYSLEXIA

TOURETTES SYNDROME

DYSCALCULIA

AUTISM

OCD

You may also have some of these as part of your neurodivergent profile.

The world would be very, very boring if we didn't have neurodivergent people in it. For example, Alexander Graham Bell was neurodivergent, and he invented the first telephone. Can you imagine a world without phones?!

Other famous people include:

- Simone Biles – amazing gymnast.
- Cara Delevingne – model and actress.
- Sam Thompson – winner of *I'm a Celebrity*.
- Greta Thunberg – environmental activist.
- Will.i.am – Member of the Black Eyed Peas and music producer.
- Stephen Wiltshire – **incredible** artist.

This list could go on and on, but we don't have enough space. Basically, the point is that all these people are neurodivergent but became incredibly successful and did not allow the fact that they were neurodivergent to hold them back. In fact, being neurodivergent probably helped make them so successful.

Being autistic means that you experience, see and feel the world differently from non-autistic or neurotypical people.

You may have difficulty with social situations and find it hard to understand what people are talking about if they are not being really clear. It may be difficult for you to 'read between the lines' during conversations or notice if people are being sarcastic, or you may find it hard to process too much information at once. As a PDAer, you may be super sensitive to other people's nonverbal communication and pick up tiny changes in the tone of their voice or facial expressions and think they are angry with you when they are not.

You will almost certainly have some sensory differences, too. You may find certain noises difficult or even unbearable. Perhaps you hate the texture of certain clothing or food. And you may notice smells that other people don't.

Everyone who is autistic is unique and different and your autism doesn't define you. It is just part of who you are.

It is also really important to know that there is **nothing wrong** with you if you are autistic. If you are struggling, it is probably because the environment you are in is wrong for you. A good way to think of this is that some people are left-handed, so 'normal' scissors are difficult for them to use. It doesn't mean that there is anything 'wrong' with left-handed people – they just need scissors that are designed differently.

CYCLES OF ANXIETY

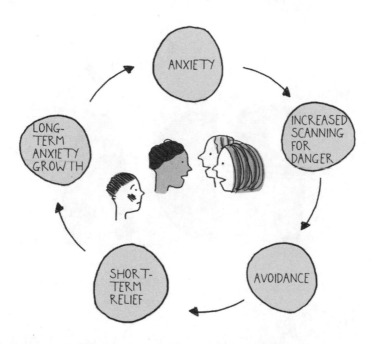

You probably find being told what to do really difficult or even impossible because it makes you feel out of control or anxious. You probably prefer to do things on your own terms and in your own time, and being in control of situations is probably really important, if not essential, to you.

STRONG INTERESTS

AUTISTIC

HUMOUR

Sensory

PDA

CHARISMATIC

AUTONOMOUS

ANXIOUS

COMMUNICATION

When you are told, asked or expected to do something by others, this may make you feel really anxious or angry, and you may react in a way that other people feel is a lot or unreasonable.

When you are asked or expected to do something, you may not always just refuse or say, 'No!' You may think of excuses, delay, procrastinate, negotiate, ignore, argue – anything to make sure you don't have to do what you have been asked or expected to do. This means that sometimes people think you are being really difficult because they think you are choosing to act this way, when in fact that isn't the case at all.

Now, everyone experiences demand avoidance at times. But as a PDAer, you may feel that sometimes **you** really want to do something, but when it comes to the time to do it, you get 'stuck' or feel that you just can't do it anymore. If someone suggests doing something you like, that might make you feel like you just can't do it anymore, and this may make you feel upset, frustrated and confused. It can feel as though you have an inner battle going on inside yourself sometimes.

If my mum and dad get too excited about the things I say I want to do, it makes me not want to do it anymore. (Annie)

It is so disabling not being able to do the things I want to do as well as the things I don't want to do. For a long time, I have wanted to play the electric guitar. I love music and it is very regulating. I got a guitar for Christmas when I was 13 and I am desperate to play it, but I haven't been able to pick it up and I am 18 now. (Eliza)

Oh, the art block is IMMENSE. I have all these ideas for things to make and I have the means and the time to conceptualize them, but my brain and my hands just refuse. I could be composing music and drawing cartoons and writing stories right now, but my brain just says 'no'. It's so frustrating. Especially since I'm so passionate about all of it. (Micah)

You probably have some strong special interests and may become fascinated or obsessed with certain topics or things. One of the features of PDA is that you may become very interested or obsessed with people. This could be people you know personally or people you have seen on TV, TikTok, Instagram, etc. You may have strong feelings about people, either loving or hating them. You may spend a lot of time focusing on your special interest and find it hard to move away from this.

Another important feature of PDA is that you probably don't really see authority and hierarchy, and you will probably seek equal and authentic connections with people who are as authentic as you. This can make it really hard when other people tell you what to do just because they are older, a parent or a teacher.

The people in your life who are in a position of authority like teachers and parents may often praise you, thinking that this is helpful, but PDAers also often find praise very difficult. Praise can set up an expectation to repeat or improve a demand. It can also feel patronizing and can create a demand to respond to the praise.

As a PDAer, you will almost always need to see the point or the 'What's in it for me?' factor when you are told to do things – without these, demands and rules will feel pointless and arbitrary.

> For a long time, I could not wear anything other than PJs and Crocs. When I started climbing, I knew I had to wear different clothes and shoes to be able to do it safely. I can now wear 'normal' clothes and my sensory needs have really diminished too. (Alfie)

Here are some quotes from young people about how having PDA makes them feel.

> It really helped me when I found out I had PDA. It made me realize I am not crazy and I understand why I feel this way when I am trying to do normal things. But it does really annoy me when it stops me from doing things that I really want to do or find normal. (Alfie)

NOTHING TO DO

HOME   LAZY DAY

COZY

FUN   ACTIVITY

LEAVE THE
HOUSE

in the mood

The fact that people around you don't understand it does not make it any less real. You're not selfish, you're not bratty, you're not lazy, you're not any of the things that they're going to claim you are. There are going to be people who will understand and sympathize and there are going to be people who won't. Don't waste time on people who won't spend time believing your struggles. (Micah)

When I first heard about PDA, I sort of denied it, I thought it was dumb. Once I heard from other adults with PDA, it made sense to me, and it was very comforting. Before I knew about PDA, I thought I was lazy and dumb. When other children in school got a task to do, they just did it and I found it so hard.

Finding out I had PDA made me realize I was not a failure. Before getting my diagnosis, it was really hard for me to tell people I had PDA. Sometimes I would feel that people thought I was making excuses. Getting my diagnosis gave me the confidence to tell people I had PDA and help them understand me better. (Rose)

PDA is not just about not being able to do things. My autism means that I have really amazing ideas, but my PDA means I can't always do them. (Annie)

Growing up not knowing I had PDA, I always knew something was up. Even when I was really young, like 1 or 2, I had a feeling that I was different. It is really hard being PDA. I have a lot of rejection from people, I felt misunderstood by lots of people growing up, but I didn't understand myself either. I had no idea what was going on. Understanding my PDA has really helped me. (Eliza)

It can feel like my PDA controls me sometimes. I try to distract myself by listening to music and talking to my friends when my anxiety gets too bad. (Caitlin)

Chapter 2

Anxiety

If you are a PDAer, then it is probably an absolute given that you experience a lot of anxiety, probably **most** if not **all** the time. You may not even realize that you feel anxious as it may be that you have got used to feeling this way all the time. Also, autistic people often experience something called alexithymia or have difficulties with interoception (internal sensations), which means it can be really hard to identify what and how you are feeling.

Feeling anxious all the time can be pretty rubbish, and feeling anxious can really impact you in many ways, but understanding your anxiety can also be really helpful. Understanding your anxiety, what causes it and how it impacts you can help you and the people around you who support you, too.

Anxiety can also be described as feeling:

* nervous

- scared
- triggered
- worried
- apprehensive
- fearful.

It's also helpful to understand that anxiety is not a 'bad' emotion. There is actually no such thing as a bad emotion. Anxiety kept our ancestors safe from danger or threats, and if we didn't respond to these, then we would not have survived!

If you have PDA, then having demands placed on you, being told what to do or having expectations placed on you will feel like **threats** because they take away your feeling of control and autonomy (more on this in the next chapter).

Anxiety impacts us in three ways:

1. **Cognitively** – this is the way that we think. The way we think about things can make us feel anxious, and when we feel anxious, we tend to think in unhelpful patterns too.

2. **Physiologically** – this is what is happening inside our bodies. Common physiological symptoms of anxiety include dry mouth, rapid heartbeat, stomach ache and not being able to think clearly.

3. **Behaviour** – when we are anxious, our behaviour will be affected. Common behaviour responses to anxiety are fight (lashing out or shouting), flight (running away), freeze, flop (legs not working or curling up into a ball) and fawn (being overly nice or friendly to the threat to keep them on your side). Your response to anxiety will be different to other people's and may differ according to the situation that you are in.

> When I feel anxious, I get a spike. I have physical feelings, my heart hurts and my chest too. I feel tense, I notice it more as I get older. My anxiety has always been really bad. I feel anxious nearly all the time, but as I learn about PDA, it is getting better. (Eliza)

COGNITIVELY

PHYSIOLOGICALLY

BEHAVIOUR

If you have PDA, then the more anxious you feel, the less you can manage demands, and the less anxious you feel, the more you will be able to manage demands.

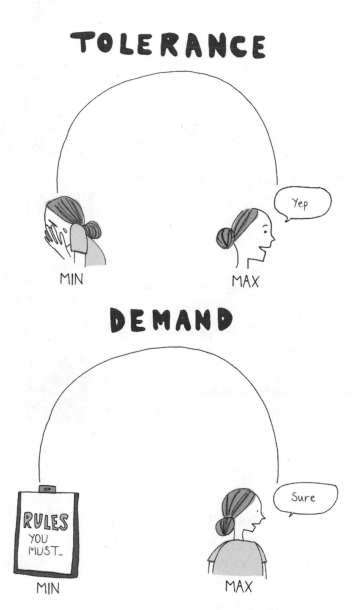

Another good way to demonstrate and understand this is to use **the bucket analogy**.

Throughout the day, we all have to manage demands, sensory issues, stresses and triggers.

Imagine these things as drops of a liquid that go into a bucket every time you have to deal with them.

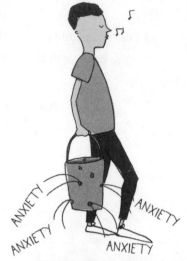

NEUROTYPICAL

Neurotypical people are pretty good at filtering these things out of their bucket, because their bucket has holes in it. It takes something big or unusual for their bucket to fill up.

Now your bucket, because you have PDA, does not have holes in it, so throughout the day, as your bucket is filling up with demands, sensory issues, stresses and triggers, it just keeps filling up because the liquid has nowhere to go. Your bucket is probably never empty

PDA

either, so the capacity of your bucket is probably less than an NT person's to start with.

Once your bucket is full, you won't have any capacity left, so even the tiniest demand will become impossible for you to manage.

Finding ways to empty your bucket or put more holes in it can be really helpful. Everyone is different, and you will hopefully find your own way to manage when your anxiety becomes too high.

> **I used to talk to my horse, rather than a person, about my worries. (Annie)**

We have drawn some blank buckets on the next page, so if you want to, you can use these to show what fills your bucket up, and also some ideas of what empties your bucket too. This is completely up to you – it's your book!

Being a teenager can be a time when you experience increased anxiety anyway. Your brain is changing and growing, and the chemicals in your brain will be all out of whack sometimes.

Your brain has two main neurotransmitters called dopamine and serotonin (don't worry, we won't be delivering a science lesson here and there is plenty of information online if you want to look this up yourself).

Dopamine levels go up during adolescence and serotonin levels go down, and this can really impact your mood. It can be helpful just knowing that there is a biological 'reason' that you feel anxious sometimes. Sometimes it is hard to find that reason – you just feel horribly anxious.

Some people take medication to help with their anxiety. This can help balance out the chemicals and help you feel less anxious. It does not have to be forever, but it can help you think more rationally while you go through a difficult time. You can speak to your parent or doctor about this if you think medication may help you. Medication is not always the answer, though, and not everyone chooses to take it. It is certainly not a 'cure' for PDA.

I have tried many meds for anxiety, but for me, personally, they did not work for long enough. It's like my body pushes them out, it's like a demand on my body to take them. It was like my soul was in a cage. My brain is very busy. Living with the disorders and accepting them is so much more helpful than taking the meds. (Eliza)

You may also find it helpful to discuss your anxiety with an adult outside of your home if you feel you can't always share this with a parent. There are counsellors and therapists out there who understand PDA, but you can also find support from other adults or mentors who really understand your PDA. This doesn't always have to be a trained counsellor or therapist, but someone who you feel really safe with. Just speaking about your worries can sometimes be helpful, but you should never feel pressured into doing this, and it can sometimes be better to work out or investigate yourself what helps you, rather than having someone tell you what to do when you are anxious.

As someone with PDA, being told how to manage your anxiety won't work! It is best that you find the things that work best for you, so it doesn't feel like a demand, but here are some things that may help you.

> Teachers would sometimes say, 'When you go into a PDA thing, can you give us a sign or signal?' But then this becomes impossible because it becomes a demand. (Rose)

> My PDA can make me avoid every coping mechanism, you know? And it's hard to vent about it to other people because every solution they offer becomes 'Well, I can't do that now'. (Micah)

Just being able to tell people you feel anxious so they know they need to back off or help you can be very beneficial, but you're not likely to say, 'Sorry, Mum/Dad/Sir/Miss, I am feeling terribly anxious at the moment. Would you mind awfully giving me the required space?' So, having a code, a signal or an agreement can make it much easier for you to get what you need.

It can be helpful to use scaling like this one:

ANXIETY SCALE

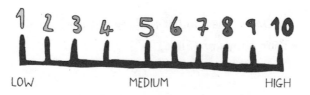

1 2 3 4 5 6 7 8 9 10

LOW   MEDIUM   HIGH

And then saying 'I am on a 9' will tell people you are really anxious and need some space.

Or just having an agreement that going in your room, blasting your music on or getting into bed means 'My bucket is full – leave me alone' can also be helpful.

The other thing to say is that when we feel really anxious, our brains stop processing information so well. Giving yourself that time and space to calm down and making sure the people around you understand and respect that are also important.

Something else that PDAers are often very good at is masking. This means that you may try to hide your anxiety. You may also try to hide your true authentic self because you don't feel safe or comfortable to show it for hours at a time, but then after being in an environment where you don't feel safe or authentic, you feel completely exhausted.

Masking can be also called fitting in, hiding, camouflaging or fawning. Fawning is when we 'people please' to fit in and we neglect our own needs in preference of other people's.

The safer you feel in situations, and the more comfortable you are with people, the more authentic you can be and the less you need to mask.

> A lot of PDAers are good at making out they are doing better than they are. (Eliza)

If you mask for too long, then eventually your mask will slip, and because it is so exhausting, you may risk going into burnout, which we talk about in Chapter 10.

Finally, you may do things when you are anxious like shout, swear or lash out that you wouldn't usually want to do. Don't beat yourself up if this happens. Remember that you are not perfect, and you are allowed to make mistakes. We all do – and the best thing about making mistakes is that we can learn from them.

When you have been very anxious, and your 'bucket' has filled up, you will probably need to be left alone and given space and time to 'cool down'. A good way to describe this is to use **the kettle analogy**.

Imagine a kettle that you fill up and boil in the morning. The water in the kettle will take a couple of minutes to boil, but will take a long time – maybe 45 minutes to an hour – to go back to room temperature again.

When you have become very anxious and stressed, it may look to other people that you have reached 'boiling point' very quickly because other people may not see the things that have been making you feel stressed and anxious. But once you have reached boiling point, it will take your adrenaline levels at least 45 minutes, and probably longer, for you to cool back down again.

If you have not been given the chance to cool down,

something may easily trigger you again, and that is like pressing the switch on a kettle when the water is still hot – it will boil almost instantly this time.

So giving yourself space and time to cool down, and helping people around you understand that you need this, is really important.

If someone tells me or suggests how to manage my anxiety, it doesn't always help. It helps me more to be left and figure it out myself. (Annie)

It's like your brain is split in two. There is a part which is forcing your body into a shutdown, and then the other part is telling you, 'Oh my god, what are you doing?' You feel guilty for the parent, or the teacher, and it isn't you that is choosing this. Your brain is trying to protect you from a threat that isn't there. Even picking up a pencil can feel like a threat. PDA rarely happens because the demand is hard, but your brain tricks you into thinking it's really hard. (Rose)

It is important to work out what works for you – if you tell someone how to work with their anxiety, it becomes a demand. Tough love never works for me, and it makes me shut down. (Rose)

I have accepted my anxiety now as something that I will always have. It will always be there, but being in a lower-demand environment helps me. It means I will have less frequent bursts of anxiety. I am still learning to be kinder to myself, but I have a better understanding of what I can and can't tolerate to keep my anxiety as low as possible. (Micah)

Chapter 3

Autonomy

People tend to talk a lot about the need for control that people with PDA have, but many people with PDA say that autonomy is actually more important to them.

> If someone tells me to do something, I hate it. It is the most awful thing! (Eliza)

Although, officially, PDA stands for Pathological Demand Avoidance, many people prefer to use the terms Persistent Drive for Autonomy (which was coined by Dr Wenn Lawson) or Pervasive Desire for Autonomy (which was coined by Tomlin Wilding).

Having autonomy or being autonomous means that you are self-governing or self-driving. If you have lots of autonomy, it probably means that you feel like you are in control, because nothing or nobody is telling you what to do or trying to control you.

When you have PDA, and autonomy is so important to you, it can feel really difficult if people start telling you what to do, or expecting you to do things in a certain way or at a certain time.

Even occasions like birthdays and Christmas can be really demanding, because you feel like you have to act in a certain way and follow certain routines and rituals, and this takes away your autonomy.

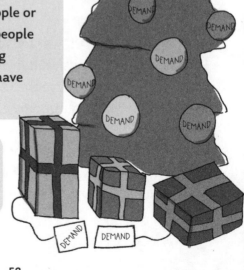

> Everything needs to be independent of other people or it can't happen. If other people start needing or expecting something of me, then I have to back out. (Micah)

> I can't have surprise presents for birthdays and Christmas. (Alfie)

> My favourite time is when I'm just left to my own devices – I love it. When people tell me or expect me to do things, it can feel awful. (Caitlin)

Because you are autistic, you may need to find a balance between having autonomy and also knowing what is going to happen.

> I like having things planned, but I need to be involved in the planning. I hate it when people make all the plans for me. (Annie)

> Autonomy is really important to me. Autonomy in PDA is different from person to person, and you need to learn what works for you. (Rose)

You probably feel that there are demands coming at you from lots of different directions in different parts of your life.

Your parents may tell you to do things like 'Go and have a bath' or 'Go and get ready for bed' or 'Come and eat your dinner'.

If you are at school or college, you probably feel that your teachers and tutors are constantly telling you to do things and putting demands on you. Even your timetable is a type of demand as it tells you where you need to be and at what time. There is no doubt about it, school is a **very** demanding place!

MEAL TIME

TIDY YOUR ROOM

School

BRUSH TEETH

BREAK TIME

LEAVE HOUSE

FAMILY OUTING

HOMEWORK

GET DRESSED

Sometimes demands are 'silent' because people have expectations of you. Just **knowing** you have to do something, like clean your teeth or get dressed, may make you feel like you are stuck.

And PDA can make life **really** hard when you want to do things but then feel like you can't, which we spoke about in the last chapter.

> Sometimes my PDA means I cannot do things I want to do. There was a time when I really wanted to get in the shower, but I just couldn't do it. My mum even offered me money to have a shower, and that made me feel worse.
>
> I eventually managed to force myself to have a shower, and then I realized that it was not as bad as I thought it would be. It helped when everyone stopped the expectation of having a shower, including myself. I also used some body wipes, which helped. I felt awful when I could not have a shower. I felt horrendous. It made me really dislike myself very badly. (Alfie)

You may be excited about doing something or going somewhere, and then just feel like you can't do it. That must be super frustrating for you but is something a lot of people with PDA experience.

If you would like to, you can record in the box that follows how it makes you feel when you get told or expected to do something.

When you have PDA, demands feel like a threat to your autonomy. People may think that you are choosing not to do what they have asked or suggested, when the fact is that you simply CAN'T do it because the demands make you feel so anxious.

IT IS CAN'T NOT WON'T

As someone with PDA, you may feel that lots of rules are meaningless, and you may not be able to understand the point of them.

It can be hard to let people know when you feel **that** they are telling you what to do. Instead of saying this directly, you may have one of the anxiety responses that we talked about in the last chapter. You may shout, swear, run away, ignore, distract and delay, and sometimes that means you may get into more trouble, which is pretty unfair, to be honest!

It may be helpful to find a way to explain to people that you are finding their demands difficult.

You could try using the following templates:

> **When you** tell me to go and have a bath,
>
> **I feel** really annoyed and angry.
>
> **I need you to** let me choose the time that I have a bath myself.

It may be really helpful for you to tell your parents that you are going to try to use the above template and practise using it with them before you are in a situation where you actually need to use it. It may be hard to say these words, so sometimes texting or messaging may be an easier way to communicate how you feel.

Of course, you may absolutely hate that idea and may not feel it would work for you – and that's fine. Perhaps this is when you could use some of the ideas mentioned in Chapter 2 on anxiety, and you could just say, 'I am on a 9!', which could be a way to tell people that you feel overwhelmed and need them to back off and give you some space.

As a PDAer, it is probably really important to you that you find your own path, but remember that the adults around you love you and want to support you, and they may need to gently guide you back on to a safer route. This is because they have your best interests at heart – even if it doesn't always feel like it! You probably need to know **why** you are being asked to do something, so don't be afraid to ask.

It is important to know that some demands are there to keep you safe, and we will cover this in Chapter 9.

Chapter 4

Rejection Sensitivity Dysphoria

Lots of people who are neurodivergent will experience something called Rejection Sensitivity Dysphoria, which is also known as RSD.

RSD means that you may feel easily rejected by people. You may interpret some comments as criticism and find this really difficult, even painful. That means you may react in a way that other people think is an overreaction, when it is not because you are having really **big** feelings about that situation.

> I think PDAers can be especially sensitive to rejection. We are just so much more sensitive anyway. I have experienced rejection from all directions because I feel that people don't understand my PDA. (Eliza)

I'd never heard of RSD until I was 17. It has been so helpful to understand it and why I react the way I do, although I am still trying to figure it out. (Caitlin)

RSD means that you may text or message a friend, and when you don't hear back from this person, you immediately think, 'That's it, they hate me!', which can make you feel really anxious. This in turn may make you ask for reassurance, and that can make you feel like you are being annoying.

RSD can make you doubt yourself and your relationships with others. It can make you feel really rubbish!

My sister has EDS [Ehlers-Danlos Syndrome], which means she is always tired in the morning and during the day, so I often feel that she is in a mood. This meant I was always saying sorry to her for things that hadn't

> happened or were out of my control. Even when she is in a good mood and happy to listen to me speaking about my special interests, I get worried she is listening to me to humour me and I will just stop speaking. (Alfie)

RSD can make navigating friendships and relationships difficult at times. But there are ways to beat it.

> Rejection sensitivity has really impacted my friendships. I may have a friend blow me out one time or give me a 'look' and I will go into panic and think, 'That's it, I need to find new friends.' (Rose)

As we explained in the earlier chapters, when you have PDA, you are probably already really sensitive to people's tone of voice and facial expressions. You may think people are angry with you or shouting at you when they are not or don't mean to.

This can set up a nasty vicious circle!

A good way to explain RSD is to imagine two smoke alarms.

One is set to the 'right' sensitivity and only goes off if there is smoke or fire in your house.

One is set so that it is too sensitive, and it will go off even if someone walks past your house smoking a cigarette. You are like that smoke detector, so you feel things like

Too sensitive...

other people's emotions and feelings really, really strongly.

If you think someone is shouting, or being unkind, it may be helpful for you to think, 'Hmm, perhaps my internal smoke alarm is being a bit too sensitive here. Maybe this person doesn't mean to shout or be unkind.'

You can also try to imagine that your brain is lying to you and trying to trick you. So, remind yourself that sometimes your brain plays these silly tricks on you and the messages it is giving you are actually false. You just need to trick it back!

If you message a friend and they don't text you back straight away, try to think of the other reasons that this might be the case. For example:

- Maybe they are asleep.
- Maybe their battery has run out.
- Maybe they are on their Xbox.

Rather than the automatic thought of 'They don't like me anymore!'

You may also be able to think of times when you thought someone was ignoring you and then it turned out they weren't – there was a very valid reason for them not responding straight away. This gives you some evidence that your brain is a bit of a fibber at times!

> I have learned that what is helpful is to sit down and really think about what happened before. I told the friend what happened in a really calm way. When I did this, my friend gave their reasons and then it was all good. You should not feel ashamed to feel what you think. You have to be aware of your condition. (Rose)

You can also explain to your friends that you have RSD, and drop them a text saying something like 'Hey! Is everything OK? I haven't heard from you for a while, and this is making me have RSD :-)', and if you have a good friend, they may just message you back with some reassurance.

Chapter 5

Friendships and Relationships

Friendships

Most people with PDA are pretty sociable and like to be around other people. But friendships can be tricky when you have PDA, for a few reasons.

> I am quite good with people, but friendships are demanding and come with lots of expectations. Knowing yourself is helpful. I am so open about my PDA, it is my entire being. (Eliza)

You are autistic, so social communication can be difficult for you to understand sometimes. You may find it hard to tell when people are joking or being sarcastic. It may be hard to 'read between the lines' and work out what people are really trying to say.

When you have PDA, you can be super sensitive to people's tone or facial expressions, so you may feel people are shouting at you or feeling angry towards you when they do not mean to be.

You may find crowded places difficult because of your sensory needs, so you may prefer not to go to busy places such as parties or shopping centres where your friends like to go.

I want friends, but I have a lot of social anxiety. Finding climbing as a hobby has really helped me to make more friends as we share an interest and I find it easier to be with friends in an environment that meets my sensory needs. Being in that crowded situation at the climbing gym has made me have to get used to it. (Alfie)

Because you have a need for autonomy, you may find it hard if you have a friend who is being bossy or controlling, or not doing the things that you would like to do.

Friendships can be demanding at times. You may find it hard to meet the demands of things like replying to text messages, or perhaps if your friends are having their own difficulties, the demand of supporting them may be really overwhelming for you, too.

All the above may make you feel that you are not a good friend, but it is important to remember that it is not your fault you find these things hard, and you can only do your best.

I don't socialize with people my age much since I'm not in school. The main person I talk to is my boyfriend. I think PDA has a lot to do with that. I'm good at making kids my age like me fast, but I easily lose contact with them.

My phone is full of numbers of people I met in a coffee shop or an event or at my job ONE time and who I had a lovely conversation with and then just never spoke to ever again.

I have a lot of friends who I met online through shared interests, and then I have a couple of close family friends a bit older than me who I've known since I was in nappies who are like cousins to me, but that's pretty much it. Basically, I'm great at making friends but I'm terrible at keeping them. (Micah)

It may be helpful for you to tell your friends that you have PDA and that there is a very real reason that you find things hard at times. When your friends understand your needs, they may be able to support you when you need it.

You may not want to tell people you have PDA, and that is fine, too. If you are only just learning about your own PDA, you may not be ready to tell other people about that just yet.

So, you could use the assertiveness technique in the last chapter to explain how you feel:

When you change our plans at the last minute,

I feel anxious.

I need you to try to give me a bit more notice, please.

Or you could use this one as an alternative:

- **Fact:** I am autistic/a PDAer and I find noisy clubs really overwhelming.
- **Sympathy:** I know you enjoy going to these places.
- **Solution:** Could I meet you before we go to the club and go somewhere a bit quieter?

Also, remember that friendships naturally have their ups and downs. Everyone has disagreements and fallings-out sometimes. Not all friendships last for ever. You may have short, intense friendships with people and then decide that the friendship is not for you anymore. Don't blame yourself when you have an argument or stop being friends with someone – remember, it takes two!

You may have friends that you have made online. Lots of autistic individuals find it easier to make friendships and connections online through gaming and social media. It can feel easier to communicate with people online rather than in person.

Social media has lots of positives, but it can have lots of negatives, too. Don't believe everything that you see and read on social media – people post what they want you to see and believe, and probably spend hours making a post to create a perfect 'snapshot' of their life!

And if you post on social media and don't get the response you were hoping for, or nasty comments or reactions, try not to take it personally. Some people enjoy baiting others and getting a reaction, so don't give them the satisfaction!

Remember, you can always turn your devices off if it all gets too much and give yourself a social media break.

During my sessions with young people with PDA, we have talked about the fact that there are always two sides to everything, but when we are autistic, it can be hard to see other people's points of view.

I have used this optical illusion as a useful reminder of this.

DUCK OR RABBIT?

It shows us that there can be two ways to look at the same situation. If you are finding it hard to see something from someone else's point of view, it may be helpful to think 'Duck/Rabbit!'

Sometimes you may find yourself in a friendship or relationship that doesn't make you happy. You may find it difficult to walk away from this person, even though you know the friendship is not good for you. This can be really hard to do. But ask yourself this: would you eat a meal that would fill you up for a short while but would then definitely make you sick? Probably not!

If you feel that a friendship is not good for you, then even though it may hurt initially, it may be best to end that friendship, put some boundaries in place and then focus on more positive friendships and relationships.

> **With friendships, if you tell someone the deep stuff and they just walk away, they are not your friend. A true friend will support you. The sad reality is that you find out who your friends are when things are hard. (Caitlin)**

Boundaries in friendships can be hard to establish, but they help you put your own needs before other people's. Examples of boundaries in friendships include:

- Not being afraid to say 'no' if something does not feel right.
- Creating time and space for yourself when you need it and prioritizing your own needs.

Here are some things you can say to help you put some boundaries in place in your friendships:

- Not taking on other people's problems if they weigh you down too: 'I understand you're having a hard time and I want to be there for you, but I don't have the emotional capacity to listen right now.'
- Telling people when you feel uncomfortable: 'It makes me feel uncomfortable when you [touch or action]. If you can't respect my space, I'll have to leave.'

- 'Please ask me first before borrowing my [possession]' or 'I would appreciate it if you didn't touch my [material thing].'

It may feel really hard when you first start asserting yourself like this, but it will get easier as you do it more and people will learn to respect your boundaries. If they don't, maybe they are not right for you!

> It can be really hard to put boundaries in place, but the first time I did it, it felt like a weight had been lifted off me. (Caitlin)

You can read more about how to set boundaries at:

www.scienceofpeople.com/how-to-set-boundaries

Relationships

At some point, you may decide that you would like to have a boyfriend or girlfriend.

As with friendships, relationships can be demanding, and as someone with PDA, the feelings you develop for someone could be very intense and overwhelming at times.

When you decide you want to pursue a relationship with someone, it can be really hard to find a way to let that person know you like them, and it can be really scary to put your feelings out there knowing that they may not be reciprocated.

Similarly, it can also be tricky to let someone know you like them, while not becoming 'too much' for them, too.

When you are in a relationship with someone, you may also find it difficult to manage their demands and needs.

> I had a boyfriend for a while, but he became very 'needy' and that became a huge demand for me. (Annie)

Chuck in a good sprinkling of the old RSD and relationships can become a bit of a minefield!

There can be lots of demands associated with relationships, but when you find the right person, relationships are absolutely worth it!

The one most important thing to remember when you embark on any kind of relationship is to stay authentic and true to yourself.

> One of the key things in relationships is two-way, honest communication. It can be really confusing when you get mixed messages. (Caitlin)

If you enter a relationship trying to hide who you are, then the other person won't be getting into a relationship with the 'real' you, and this will not create a solid foundation for your future time together.

As a PDAer, authenticity is probably very important to you anyway.

> I am very open about being PDA. When you have worked all this stuff out, you can go into relationships

and friendships more openly. I need clear-cut communication and honesty. You won't embarrass me – just be honest with me! Honesty and understanding are essential. I have no energy for bullshit! (Eliza)

And remember, you are amazing as you are, so don't try to change to be what someone else wants you to be!

If you feel comfortable doing so, then it may be helpful to explain to a future partner that you have PDA. This means they will understand your needs better. It can be complicated to explain PDA and may take some time for your potential partner to fully understand you and your needs.

When a relationship breaks down and it is not your choice, it can be incredibly hard. As a PDAer, you may feel that you have lost all your autonomy in the relationship because you did not want it to end. It can feel very painful and hurtful.

Allow yourself to feel safe and process the loss. Try to remember that you are not in control of other people's feelings. If there is someone you trust, then you can speak to them about this. It will hurt for a while, but allow yourself to grieve the loss and it **will** get easier in time. Remember, when one person leaves your life, it creates a space for someone new!

Chapter 6

Gender and Sexuality

The teenage years are a time when you will probably naturally explore and question your gender and sexuality. Research has shown that gender diversity is much higher in the neurodivergent community than in the neurotypical community.

You may feel that you don't want to conform to the demands of gender stereotypes.

> As a PDAer, we are just questioning the default of what we should be in terms of our sexuality and gender. We get told we should be these things, but the reality is we are not the default. (Eliza)

Your gender and sexuality are something that you should be allowed to work out on your own, in an autonomous way. You may feel that it is a demand to 'come out' or discuss this with your family, too. You may be worried about their reaction or worried that they will want to speak about it with you in depth, which you may not want to do.

> The demand of having an awkward conversation with my mum stopped me from coming out as bi sooner. (Alfie)

> I haven't told both my parents that I am bi. (Anon)

> The demand to come out is really big. I think I may be a lesbian, but I worry about my family knowing this. There is also pressure from my friends. This is why I don't talk about it with my friends. (Anon)

It can be very difficult and confusing to work out your own identity, and you may feel pressure from others to conform and be a certain way. Again, as a PDAer, authenticity is probably very important to you, so take your time, chat to people who you feel safe to discuss this with and do your own research.

> Lots of trans people feel that it is a demand to conform to a certain gender. When I was a little girl, I felt like I wasn't girly enough, then when I first came out as a trans man, I felt like I wasn't manly enough. Now I'm just doing whatever I find most comfortable. I want to start on testosterone ASAP and get top surgery

and I'm not really bothered with pronouns, but I feel comfortable presenting more masculine.

Sexuality-wise, I knew I liked both men and women from a VERY young age. I'm now comfortably out as bisexual and have been in a very happy relationship with a gay trans man for over a year now. (Micah)

Whatever relationship you find yourself in, think ASC:

Authentic – always be true to your authentic self. You are great as you are, so don't change for anyone else.

Safe – always keep yourself safe.

Comfortable – don't do anything that makes you feel uncomfortable. You could use your boundaries which we covered in the friendships section of Chapter 5.

Here are some books that you may wish to look up on these topics:

- *Queerly Autistic: The Ultimate Guide for LGBTQIA+ Teens on the Spectrum* by Erin Ekins
- *The Awesome Autistic Guide for Trans Teens* by Yenn Purkis and Sam Rose
- *The Autistic Trans Guide to Life* by Yenn Purkis and Wenn Lawson

Chapter 7

Family Life

As the saying goes, 'You can choose your friends, but you can't choose your family!' Mums and dads, brothers and sisters can be really annoying sometimes, and it can be hard when you all have to share the same space. Extended family like grandparents, aunts, uncles and cousins may not always understand you and your needs either.

Remember that ALL families have arguments and conflicts – this is completely normal.

As a PDAer, autonomy is important to you, and that can make relationships with family members hard. If a friend is annoying, you have the choice to walk away, but in a family home, that is not always possible. You may also feel forced into family situations at times.

> My sister tries to talk to me about her issues, but sometimes I find that a demand. (Annie)

You may feel as you get older that your parents are asking or telling you to do things that feel unfair or pointless. As they place demands on you, this will trigger your anxiety and you may feel the need to get away from them, shout or maybe even lash out physically.

It can be really helpful to you to have a safe space that you can go to if you feel overwhelmed or your emotions are getting too big.

> Family life can be really complicated and demanding sometimes. If I didn't have my own space, it would be impossible! I feel very protective about my own space, and I need people to respect that. (Caitlin)

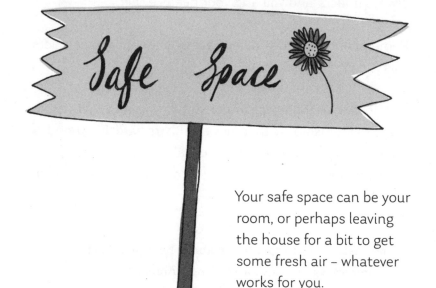

Your safe space can be your room, or perhaps leaving the house for a bit to get some fresh air – whatever works for you.

As a family, you could agree that when you are in that safe space, people leave you alone until you are ready to speak to them. It would be best to discuss this when things are calm so that you can put it into practice when things are not. You can also agree on a safe space when you go out or visit your extended family, too.

> There are demands in the household that I can freeze over. Sometimes I get upset and I leave the room and go to my room, and then I get upset and stroppy and I may go downstairs again, but I can't go back in the room. I wait in the kitchen, and I need my family to come to me. I know it sounds selfish. When I was younger, I used to break stuff – this would help me feel like I was breaking free, but I was not happy when I did it. (Rose)

You may also find it easier to 'speak' to your family in less direct ways when you need to communicate with them, particularly when communicating difficult feelings. It may be easier to send text or WhatsApp messages, or to send a written note.

You could also use lots of the ideas we suggested in

Chapter 5 about expressing how you feel. This will help you express yourself in an assertive way.

You could also try using the ideas we have suggested in Chapter 3 such as:

When you tell me I have to be home by 10 pm,

I feel really angry.

I need you to help me understand why I need to be back home by this time.

And:

- **Fact:** My friends are allowed out later than me.
- **Sympathy:** I know you worry about me.
- **Solution:** I could get a lift back at 11 pm and will phone you at 10 pm to let you know I am safe.

Another thing that can be really helpful in avoiding conflict is learning to compromise or meet in the middle. Again, it is probably best to practise doing these things when you and your family members feel calm.

We live in an adapted house, but it is a lot sometimes. From when I was 16 and I read about PDA, I have worked a lot of things out for myself. I am constantly analyzing everything. The thing that has helped me to understand myself is thinking about situations: Who,

What, Where and Why? It can help you work out your feelings. It feels quite demanding at first, but it has really helped me. After doing this for a couple of years, I don't have to think about the questions anymore – it just gives me answers. (Eliza)

It can help to see things visually, particularly when you are autistic. Venn diagrams can be helpful to lay out what you like and want to do, versus what others like and want to do. The stuff in the middle is what you both like, and the other bits are what you and others like separated out. Using this can be helpful when agreeing on what to do with siblings or even things like what you want to eat. An example of a Venn diagram is shown below. There are blank versions for your use in the Appendix at the back of the book.

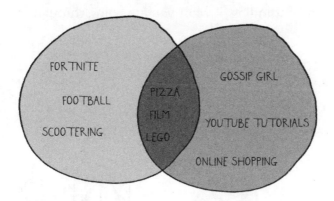

It may also be really helpful for your family members to have a better understanding of your PDA. So, it may help the whole family if they can find a way to learn about PDA and how it impacts you. This could include siblings and grandparents, too.

It may be helpful to have a phrase that you can use to tell people you have PDA. You could say something like 'I have a type of autism called PDA. This means I feel very anxious a lot of the time and find it hard when people put demands on me.'

You could also let people know the most important thing about your needs, such as 'I find it really hard to eat at the dinner table with lots of people. So I will eat on my own and then come back and join you all later.'

Remember that your parents and grandparents may seem old, but they have been teenagers too, so they will have **some** understanding of what you are going through!

With a friend, you can walk away, but it is hard to walk away from family. I feel like my mum over-explains things, and I feel bad, but her talking too much makes me feel stressed. But I feel stressed telling her to stop talking so much, too. All my family are ND [neurodivergent], so it can be hard to balance all our individual needs sometimes. I love chatting to my nan as she loves listening to me speak about random things and she always seems very interested. Shared interests and shared humour are really important. (Alfie)

Since I got my diagnosis, it has definitely helped our family and things have definitely improved. You can be feeling guilty about your behaviour and how it is impacting the other person, but you cannot stop it, and you know that if you were in their position, you would be feeling the same thing. Remember, there is no such thing as the perfect family. (Rose)

Chapter 8

School and Education

There is no doubt about it, school can be incredibly difficult when you have PDA, because school is an incredibly demanding place! Schools can also be really difficult from a sensory perspective as they can be noisy and smelly. Schools also require you to be able to manage lots of transitions, too.

As 70 per cent of children with PDA don't go to school, it is likely that you are home-educated, have an Educated Other Than At School (EOTAS) programme if you are in the UK, or go to an alternative provision. Perhaps you are in school or college, and they are supporting you really well – if that is the case, then that is brilliant and long may it continue!

> School is just not for people with PDA, really. The way the system is set up is just not very helpful. Learning about your brain is helpful. For any PDA learning, it is best to go your own way. (Eliza)

You may feel like you are carrying a huge load of demands and anxiety when you enter a learning environment, and there may be lots of days when you feel that you just can't go.

Also, as someone with PDA, you will probably find it hard to recognize hierarchy and authority, so it can make it difficult to be in an environment where you have to do things just because people tell you that you should!

School, college and other learning environments are full of rules and expectations. As a PDAer, a lot of these rules will seem meaningless to you because you need to see the point of them.

Lots of the young people I have worked with over the years found primary school OK, but then found the transition into secondary school really hard. One of the reasons for this is that, as a PDAer, you need autonomy, and the secondary system doesn't give you that. There are also a lot more transitions in secondary school, and secondary schools are usually much bigger, so harder from a sensory perspective, too.

I was at a mainstream school at primary, and because I was quite smart, there was so much perfectionism, I was top of my year for everything, and this caused me so much anxiety. My anxiety was more prevalent when I was at school and going full-time. When I was 15, I was doing an hour a week of school and my anxiety was still so high all the time. (Eliza)

The education system is a little bit like an egg-timer in terms of the autonomy you have. As you go through the system you have less autonomy and more demands placed on you, and that can be really hard to manage when you have PDA.

Hopefully, if you are in school or have a tutor, they understand you have PDA and they understand your needs. Because you are autistic, your school or place of learning has to make 'reasonable adjustments' to ensure that you can learn as well as your peers. Here are some examples of reasonable adjustments for someone with PDA:

- working in a quiet space if you don't want to work in the classroom
- having extra time to complete work, exams and homework (if you have to do it)
- having a reduced timetable
- being given choices of tasks
- sitting fewer exams than your peers
- using a laptop or computer rather than having to write.

We have put more examples of how adults can support you in the learning environment in the Appendix at the back of the book so that you can show your teacher or tutor to understand what it is that you need.

Teachers often ask me what they can do to make it easier for me at school. Although I have been living with this my whole life, it is hard to explain. I need teachers to be understanding and understand PDA is a real thing. After I have been anxious, I need people to listen to me. Sometimes I don't know what I want or what I need them to do. The rational side of my brain is still trying to figure out what is going on. If teachers pay very close attention to my body language, it can help. If I go silent, then this means that I am getting very anxious. Body language is very important to read because I can't really talk when I am anxious. (Rose)

As an autistic person, you may have very strong interests and probably prefer to learn things about them rather than the things that you are just not interested in. If you are in school, then your parents may be able to ask for you to have a flexible timetable and it can be helpful to 'RAG' the timetable to illustrate what part of the timetable you find enjoyable and easier (Green), what parts are just a bit 'meh' (Amber) and what parts are absolutely not happening (Red)!

	MONDAY	TUESDAY	WEDNESDAY	THURSDAY	FRIDAY
	SCIENCE	MATHS Don't Like	MUSIC	PE Don't Like	MATHS Don't Like
BREAK					
	ART Like	ENGLISH	COMPUTER SCIENCE Like	SCIENCE	ENGLISH
	MATHS Don't Like	ENGLISH	ENGLISH	SCIENCE	PE Don't Like
LUNCH					
	Don't Like PE	GEOGRAPHY	Don't Like MATHS	HISTORY Like	SCIENCE
	ENGLISH	GEOGRAPHY	Don't Like MATHS Like	HISTORY Like	ART Like

which means that you are good at teaching yourself. You probably feel that you don't need a teacher because you can teach yourself! You may like to work on your own, or perhaps with a friend sometimes, too.

The two most important things that PDAers tell us that they need when they are at school or college is at least one safe person and at least one safe place where they can go if their anxiety gets too much. Can you think of who this person or people could be, and where your safe place might be, too?

> I have a mixture of school and home education. I love my school because of the people. They are kind and they understand me and treat me as an equal. I also feel popular there. (Annie)

> The most important thing I had at school was a safe and authentic connection with someone. I need people to be on my level and joke around with me. (Caitlin)

If you are in school or college or have an EOTAS package, you may be taking exams. Again, by law, your school or college has to offer you some reasonable adjustments when doing so, such as extra time and rest breaks. The school or college will have to apply for these things well in advance, though, so if you think these things will help you, speak to your parents or the school or college so that they have enough time to sort this out for you.

Also, remember that exams are not the be-all and end-all. If you feel that you can't take your exams, or you don't get the results you need, you can take them later when you feel more ready. At the end of the day, you can only do your best, and colleges and universities can sometimes be flexible on the qualifications you need to attend, depending on the course.

Coursework and homework deadlines can feel like really big demands, too. If you tell the adults who support you that you are struggling, they may be able to give you extra time, or help you chunk your work so it doesn't feel like such a big demand.

Try to be honest and open about how you are feeling so that the adults who support you know you need help.

A lot of the young people I have worked with have found college much easier than school. You get to focus on the subjects you like, you can drop the ones you hate, classes are often smaller, and you have a lot more autonomy at college, too.

There needs to be a more accessible education system. Now I have my EOTAS package, it is 100 times better than school. It is so much nicer, and I feel like I am learning at a faster rate than if I was in school. I get to pick and choose the things that I want to do. My science tutor is going to start teaching me history soon as my interest has changed and she can go with this. (Alfie)

Chapter 9

Keeping Yourself Safe

Although it can be really hard to accept demands when you have PDA, it is important to remember that some demands are there to keep you safe, even if that feels really annoying at times!

As a PDAer, there will be times when it is difficult to balance the demands of keeping yourself safe versus the demand of taking exciting risks!

It is probably safe to say that many teenagers will experiment with drugs, alcohol, smoking, vaping and sex. Most teenagers can also be susceptible to peer pressure, and people who experience RSD often become 'people pleasers'. When this

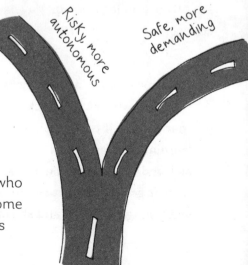

Risky, more autonomous

Safe, more demanding

happens, you can find yourself putting other people's needs before your own.

EVERYONE ELSE DOES

ALL MY MATES ARE

PEOPLE TELL ME I SHOULD

THEY SAY IT'S FUN

We are not going to tell you not to do these things, because that would be a demand! But if you are going to experiment, then it is important that you keep yourself safe.

PDAers could be susceptible to peer pressure. On the other hand, they may tell people to f**k off! When I was younger, I was masking; the older I am getting, my

> reaction is more likely to freeze. With drugs etc. when I was younger, me and my friends had a conversation about drugs, and they said they might try. My opinion was that I was not interested. We can be prone to addiction. When I want something, I want all of it. I try to keep myself away from things that I think could lead me down that path. (Eliza)

Rather than listen to other people's opinions telling you what you should or shouldn't do, it can be helpful for *you* to work out the 'What's in it for me?' to keep yourself safe and well.

For example, you may decide the 'What's in it for me?' factor for not smoking or vaping is that you will have more money to spend on your other hobbies and interests.

> I have had temptations before me, but the 'What's in it for me?' factor helps. Understanding the consequences of my actions helped. (Rose)

The 'What's in it for me?' factor for practising safe sex is that you will avoid unwanted pregnancy or sexually transmitted infections (STIs).

The 'What's in it for me?' factor for not drinking too much alcohol is that you won't feel rubbish when you wake up in the morning!

The 'What's in it for me?' factor for not taking drugs is that you won't risk getting into trouble with the police or damaging your mental health.

> If I am going to try these things, I need to try them safely so that they don't affect me in a negative way, and I don't want to impact on my mental health. (Alfie)

If you do feel peer-pressured into doing anything, then it may be helpful to have something prepared that you can say or an excuse like 'I can't drink because I am on antibiotics'. Or you could fill a glass or can with water or a soft drink and no one will know what you are drinking!

As a PDAer, control is going to be important to you, so if you are experimenting with these things and it does feel that you are losing control, or you don't feel safe anymore, then try to listen to your instincts. It may be helpful for you to speak to someone you can trust, and you may not want to speak to your parents about these things.

> I am not stupid, and I am also really vigilant and that stops me from taking stupid risks. I can talk to adults around me about these things, not always my parents. (Annie)

You may have friends that you have met online. It is important to remember that not everyone may be who they seem to be, so do be careful when sharing information about yourself, particularly if you have just met someone. Don't share photos or give away personal information about yourself, such as your address, until you are absolutely sure that someone is completely safe.

Below are some organizations that you can speak to if you feel you need a safe person to reach out to.

For drugs and addiction:

Frank: www.talktofrank.com

Online safety:

Safewise: www.safewise.com

This website has information on drugs, addiction and online safety:

Young Minds: www.youngminds.org.uk

This website has information for teens on online safety, sexual health, etc.:

Kids Health: https://kidshealth.org

Chapter 10

Moving into Adulthood

As a teenager with PDA, you may find it difficult to see yourself as a 'non-adult'. Lots of the PDAers we have worked with over the years actually already see themselves as adults, and did so even when they were children.

You may feel that you are desperate to be an adult, as you feel that you will have more control over your life and also have more autonomy.

You may feel the opposite and feel that growing up and becoming an adult is really scary, as there will be lots of demands for you to have to deal with.

Perhaps you feel a mixture of the two – and that may feel quite confusing at times!

Demands change as you get older, and you have a different type of autonomy. You can say goodbye to demands such as:

- having to go to school or have an education (unless you choose to go to university)
- having curfews
- following age restrictions.

But then you may have new demands to follow, such as:

- paying rent or a mortgage
- having a job or working
- paying bills.

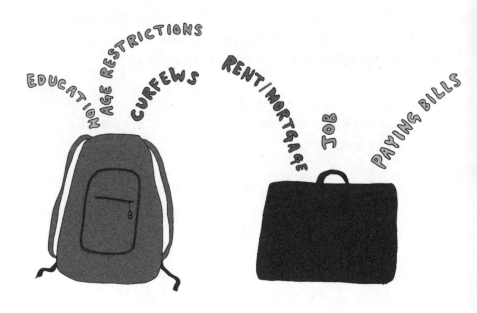

You can also gain autonomy by learning to drive, going travelling and moving away from home.

> I know I am going to have more responsibilities when I am older. I don't need constant reminders and pressure from my parents about this and need to be able to figure it out myself with support when I ask for it. (Caitlin)

As an adult with PDA, it will be important that you feel you can advocate for yourself. This will mean that you can tell people what you might struggle with, and the things that you need to help support you.

You may feel that you can tell people that you have PDA. You could say something like:

> I am a truly awesome person who also happens to be autistic. My type of autism is PDA, which stands for Pathological Demand Avoidance, and this means I find it hard to manage demands sometimes because they make me feel anxious.

Or something like:

> I am autistic. This means I am really struggling with the noise/lights/smells (delete as appropriate) in here and I need to sit somewhere else.

Being able to self-advocate will mean that you can tell people like friends, colleagues or your boss what you need so you can feel comfortable and less anxious.

You can also tell people the preferred way that they communicate with you, too:

> Because I am autistic, I find it really hard to take phone calls – would you mind sending me a WhatsApp instead?

Or:

> My PDA means I find it hard when I have too many demands placed on me. I would prefer it if you gave me more choices/more time to process/more autonomy to make my own decisions.

Once you start working, your employer will have to make reasonable adjustments for you, just like your school had to do. Because you are autistic, and autism is covered by the Equalities Act, this is something that employers legally have to do.

We have put some examples of reasonable adjustments at work in the Appendix at the back of this book which you can refer to when you start work and also maybe show your employer if you would find that helpful.

We know many adults with PDA who are self-employed, and they have found work they love which is linked to their special interests. Eliza and I are both self-employed. We work in a field that we love and feel passionate about, with people who understand us and our needs, too.

Being your own boss means also you have a lot more autonomy, and you can pick and choose when you work. There are still some rules you have to follow, such as paying

tax, so we have put a useful link about that in the Appendix at the back of the book for when the time comes.

One of the most important things that you can do to help you self-advocate is to tell people how many 'spoons' you have.

Now, this has absolutely nothing to do with cutlery!

Spoon Theory was developed by Christine Miserandino in 2003 as a way of describing how much mental energy she

SPOON THEORY

I have 12 x spoons to get through the day...

 WAKE UP =

 SHOWER =

GET DRESSED =

 BREAKFAST =

 SCHOOL =

 REMAINING SPOONS

had. Christine Miserandino had a chronic illness and found Spoon Theory a really helpful way of telling people that she was running low on energy. The term has been adopted by the neurodivergent community and is a really easy way to express how you feel when you are getting tired or feeling overwhelmed.

In Spoon Theory, one 'spoon' is like a unit of energy. So, for example, you will wake up each morning with a certain number of spoons. Demands, expectations, tasks and jobs will use up your spoons until you run out. When you are out of spoons, you will feel like you have no energy left.

Here are some examples of things that use up my spoons (everyone's list will be different, though):

- attending meetings with lots of people
- using public transport
- going to the supermarket
- reading long, boring emails
- going to busy, noisy parties.

There are lots of things that will replenish your spoons. These are the things that replenish my spoons:

- walking my dogs
- nature
- clothes shopping
- watching rubbish reality TV
- being with one or two close friends.

When you identify the things that use your spoons and give you spoons back, it can help you plan your time so that you don't run out of energy and risk burning out, which we will come to in a minute.

You may find it helpful to list some of the things that use your spoons and some of the things that give you spoons back in the table below (we have also included some spare tables in the Appendix at the back of the book for you to use in the future if you think this may be helpful).

Things that use my spoons	Number	Things that give me spoons back	Number

The best thing about Spoon Theory is that once you understand it, you can help others to understand how you are feeling. Saying to someone 'I am out of spoons' or 'I am getting low on spoons' will help them to understand that you are running low on energy and need a break or can't do any more that day.

This may be something that is really helpful for you to use at work or with your family and friends, too.

A lot of neurodivergent people experience 'burnout' when they run out of spoons. Burnout can occur after you have been in a stressful situation for too long, or when you are not allowing yourself enough time to replenish your spoons.

When you burn out, it is a bit like a phone that has too many apps open, or a computer with too many documents or programs running. Initially, the phone or computer will go slower, then eventually it will just stop working and will need to be shut down so that it can reset itself and start again.

Autistic burnout is described by autistic people in a research paper called 'Investigating autistic burnout' (2022), by Dr Samuel Arnold, Julianne Higgins and others, as 'no longer having the energy necessary to act neurotypical'. In other words, it means not having the energy or resources to keep masking and fitting in.

The main reason autistic people experience burnout is because of how exhausting and debilitating it can be to mask our differences as autistic individuals. Autistic people mask because of living in a world that is not designed for brains that are different and because, unfortunately, so many people don't understand what it really means to be neurodivergent.

If you have been in an environment that does not meet your

needs, or if you have been bullied, restrained or invalidated, then this can be traumatic and can contribute to burnout.

Burnout can also be experienced by people who are autistic, PDA or ADHD.

What is burnout like? It is often experienced as (among other things):

- feeling exhausted
- wanting to stay in bed and sleep more
- lacking motivation to do anything
- increased demand avoidance
- feeling tearful
- finding it harder to manage your emotions
- feeling detached
- feeling overwhelmed
- not wanting to eat (or overeating)
- not being able to focus or concentrate on anything
- not enjoying things you used to enjoy
- being less able to communicate
- having difficulties with memory
- being unable to do things that you used to do (e.g. look after yourself).

Autistic people often need more time to process things and that includes change.

A form of autistic burnout can be experienced on a regular and even a daily basis. This is often referred to as social hangovers or 'too much people-ing'.

But autistic burnout is often described as something that lasts for months or even longer in some people, especially if they don't get the help and support they need.

So why do autistic people experience burnout? The main causes are:

- masking your differences as an autistic person for too long
- sensory overload (noise, touch, taste, smell, sight, emotions, body functions, etc.)
- too many demands and expectations
- transitions and changes (including constant sudden changes)
- trauma.

Essentially, when the demands of an environment (which can be home, school, college, university or work) are bigger than your capacity to cope, then burnout can occur.

What helps if you are experiencing autistic burnout? Because resting can be difficult (especially if you have ADHD because our brains never stop!), when I say resting is important to help with recovery, you might think that's impossible.

But it is possible, and it doesn't just mean sleeping, although some people do sleep more when they are burnt out. Your mind especially needs to reset and recharge, just like when that mobile phone battery needs to be plugged in to recharge, or when you turn your laptop off and turn it back on again to reboot it.

Resting, rebooting and recharging are what your brain needs, as it has been in survival mode for a long time. This is exhausting and can lead to lots of struggles with mental health.

Resting can look different for different people and can include for example:

- gaming
- sleeping
- drawing
- playing a musical instrument
- listening to music
- going for a walk in nature
- being creative
- spending hours focusing on things you're passionate about
- reading
- writing songs or stories.

Whatever it is that helps you to recharge your low battery – and is not making demands on you - can be restful and helpful in burnout. It might take a long time to get to a place where things are better again, and you cannot get better if there are still lots of demands.

Everyone will experience burnout differently, but the important thing is to try to recognize when you are starting to experience the symptoms, and then be kind to yourself so that you can start to look after yourself.

Recognizing the symptoms is really important, and managing your spoons is an important part of this. Sometimes this will mean saying 'no' to other people, or even yourself.

You can try to balance out the things that cause burnout with the things that give you happiness and energy.

There is a really good workbook about autistic burnout written by Viv Dawes that we recommend called *Understanding Autistic Burnout,* which you may find helpful to work through, too.

Final Thoughts

I would rather live with my PDA than without it. It is so intertwined with everything I do. It is a huge part of who I am. People with PDA do think and learn very differently and there is definitely a place for us, but it has not really been properly established yet. In the future, we will serve a good purpose. (Rose)

I can't let my PDA define me. It is just a part of who I am. I am not going to let it hold me back in the future. (Caitlin)

I was really miserable in primary school and was diagnosed with depression when I was 7. I was kicked out of loads of schools including a school for kids who had been kicked out of school! My PDA has made life incredibly difficult at times, but as I have grown older and with massive thanks to my EOTAS provider, I have made so much progress. I have two jobs now, and I am about to start my dream job soon even though I missed all of secondary school.

I have a boyfriend who lives abroad, and in the summer, I was able to travel to visit him independently. I have been able to kick my arse into doing things I wanted to do. PDA can make it so hard to do the things you want to do, but as you grow older, it becomes possible to realize that you are in control, and you CAN do things.

I have had to make the decision to change my behaviour. It is difficult, but you can do it. I understand if you are a teenager reading this that you may think this is all crap, because this is what I used to think, but there are ways around doing things and you can do it too. I ask myself if I am happy and the answer is 'yes'. (Micah)

I was diagnosed with PDA when I was 14. I was refusing to go into school and was regularly having meltdowns when at home. When it came to exams in school, I would always fail them despite being top of the class during normal lessons. This became frustrating, and I know it is to do with the demand of taking an exam and the expectation to do well. I managed to finish school with both GCSEs and A Levels but realized university was never going to be an option.

I found myself an apprenticeship with an engineering

company. I knew an apprenticeship would be tough and would come with another load of demands and expectations, but I would have these in life anyway. My current strategies for coping would still work but may need to be adjusted slightly; my hobbies of climbing and taking the dog out to agility helped empty the bucket just as they always had.

Despite the challenges, this was definitely the right path for me, and by the time I was midway through my apprenticeship, I won the West London Business Awards' Highly Commended Apprentice of the Year. I have now completed the apprenticeship with top marks and am currently a Quality Engineer at another engineering company. (Sophie – now an adult PDAer)

Appendix

Here is a statement that you may wish to use to explain to people that you have PDA. This could include teachers, tutors, employees, friends, doctors, dentists, etc.:

> I have a type of autism known as Pathological Demand Avoidance. This means that I have high anxiety and a need for control and autonomy. I don't like to stand out or appear different to my peers.

If you want to follow a teen with PDA on social media, then you may want to check out:

> ChloeMeJustMe on YouTube or Facebook

Chloe also has some really helpful guides to PDA for teens called *My PDA Brain* Digital Downloads, which are available on Etsy (see www.etsy.com/shop/thehappymakeruk).

There are also lots of other neurodivergent people you can follow on TikTok and YouTube.

Here is some information that you can show to your teachers or tutors to help them understand your PDA and what you need from them. You could also use some of these to show your employer or colleagues when you start work:

- As someone with PDA, I experience a lot of anxiety. I may not always look anxious, but please remember my anxiety is always there. Also, my PDA stops me from doing things I want to do as well as things I don't want to do sometimes.

- Take your time to build up a relationship with me. Sometimes I may like to just sit and talk about the things I am interested in. The safer I feel with you, the less anxious I will feel, and the less anxious I feel the higher my tolerance to demands will be.

- I prefer you to use phrases such as 'I wonder if you could...' or 'Shall we see if we can...' rather than giving me direct demands and telling me what to do.

- You could also offer me choices as this gives me a feeling of control and autonomy and lowers my anxiety. For example, you could say, 'Would you like to do X or Y first?' or 'Would you like to sit here or here to do your work?'

- Be aware of your facial expressions. As someone with PDA, I can be hypersensitive to your tone of voice and facial expressions, which can often cause me more anxiety.

- I may not like to be praised directly. Direct praise can be difficult for individuals with a PDA profile as it can set up an expectation that a demand will be complied with again or even improved upon.

- When doing my school or college work, use my areas of strengths and interests to engage and motivate me, but include me in discussions about this.

- Reduce the pressures you put on me. There will be days when my anxiety is too high for me to comply with any demands you place on me. I will have good and bad days. Look for ways you can support me and share the load of demands.

- Give factual reasons to explain why you need things to be done a certain way. Don't use opinions such as 'That's dangerous' or 'You're too young to do that'.

- Show empathy and validate what I find hard. For example, acknowledging 'I know you find this work challenging. Shall we work on this together?' or 'Do you need some more time to do this?'

- Try to find a balance between routine and spontaneity because a strict routine may feel like a demand. But ensure that you involve me in planning and don't impose routines upon me.

Here are some helpful websites you can share with teachers, tutors and employers:

- **PDA Society:** www.pdasociety.org.uk
- **National Autistic Society:** www.autism.org.uk
- **Positive Assessments Support and Training:** www.p-ast.co.uk

Here are some books that your teachers, tutors or employers may find helpful in learning about PDA:

- *The Educator's Experience of Pathological Demand Avoidance* by Laura Kerbey and Eliza Fricker
- *Can I tell you about Pathological Demand Avoidance syndrome?* by Phil Christie and Ruth Fidler
- *The Teacher's Introduction to Pathological Demand Avoidance* by Clare Truman
- *A Different Way to Learn* by Dr Naomi Fisher

Here are some blank tables you can use to help you identify what uses up your spoons and what helps you replenish them. The 'number' sections will help you work out how many spoons each activity uses or gives you.

Things that use my spoons	Number	Things that give me spoons back	Number

Things that use my spoons	Number	Things that give me spoons back	Number

Here are some blank Venn diagrams that we talked about in Chapter 7 that you may find helpful to use with your siblings or other family members to work out the things that you can do together or separately.

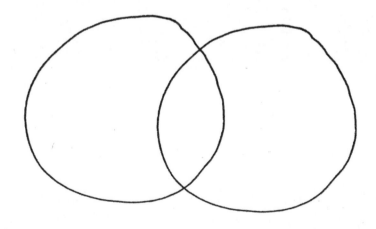

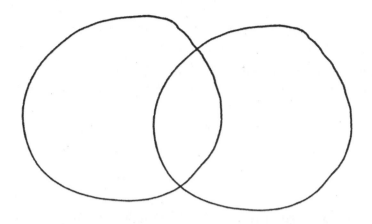

Information for work

You may not need this section now, but it may be helpful to refer to this in the future when you start working. You can also use the list above to show people how they can support you at work.

Legally, your employer will have to make adjustments to help you do your job as well as someone without a disability. The Equality Act 2010 calls these 'reasonable adjustments'.

Here are some examples of reasonable adjustments for the workplace:

- Having a quiet workspace.
- Having a quiet place to eat away from others.
- Allowing you to come into work and leave earlier or later when it is not as busy.

- Ensuring the sensory environment is not overwhelming for you.
- Keeping your camera off during online meetings.
- Communicating with you in a style you prefer (e.g. emails, not phone calls).
- Giving you special software such as dictation software.
- Allowing you extra time in interviews.

Reasonable adjustments should be made for your own unique needs.

You can read more about reasonable adjustments at work at:

www.autism.org.uk/advice-and-guidance/professional-practice/employment-adjustments-tips

Here is a useful link if you are considering becoming self-employed:

www.gov.uk/working-for-yourself

Other useful links about anxiety and mental health:

- **Young Minds:** www.youngminds.org.uk
- **Stem4:** https://stem4.org.uk
- **Kooth:** www.kooth.com